Phonetic Storybook 17

The Trophy Book

by Sue Dickson

Illustrated by Norma Portadino

Total Language Arts K-3
Reading•Writing•Spelling•Phonics•Speaking

Sing, Spell Read & Write

Printed in the United States of America

Sing, Spell, Read & Write © Copyright 1978, Sue Dickson
Virginia Beach, Virginia, 23463 • 804-523-1600

ISBN: 1-55574-020-0 (Volume 17)
ISBN: 1-55574-003-0 (17 Volume Set)
ISBN: 1-55574-000-6 (Complete Kit)

All rights reserved for all countries including the right of translation. Copying or reproducing any of the materials in this book by any means is an infringement of copyright.

Contents

                                                                  page

ph = f   **Baseball in Philadelphia** 3
                   by Lynda MacDonald

ch = k
ss = sh   **Christopher's Trip** 14
                   by Lynda MacDonald

Rulebreakers and wacky words

                 Brave Heart, the Indian Guide 36
                   by Lynda MacDonald

                 Friends 46
                   by Lynda MacDonald

ch = sh   **Charlotte and Cheryl in Chicago** 54
                   by Sue Dickson

<u>ous</u> and Multi-syllable words

                 The Enormous Surprise 56
                   by Lynda MacDonald

Raceway Step 34a

ph = f

Baseball in Philadelphia

Vocabulary

1. Joseph
2. Ralph
3. phooey
4. dolphins
5. gophers
6. Philadelphia
7. photos
8. photographs
9. autographs
10. alphabet
11. phonics
12. phonograph
13. telephone
14. trophy
15. pharmacy

It was a rainy day.
"Phooey!" said Joseph.
"Phooey!" said Ralph.

No ball game today.
Ducks and dolphins like rain,
but not gophers!

No trip to Philadelphia!
No photographs of the baseball players!

No autographs on the photos. Joseph was sad and mad. Ralph was mad and sad.

Mom said, "Do your homework. Write the alphabet."

"Learn your phonics song."

Ralph put the record on the phonograph.

The little gophers worked. They wrote the alphabet and sang the Phonics Song.

Then the telephone rang.

"Telephone!" called Mom. "It is Dad!"

11

Girls and Boys: Hold this page up to a mirror. Can you read where Dad works?

"The rain will stop.

I'll close the shop.

We have to go.

Our team's on top!"

"Come on! Let's go!
Hooray! Hooray!
Our team will win
a trophy today!"
The End

13

Raceway Step 34b

ch = k
ss = sh

Christopher's Trip

Vocabulary

ch = k

1. school
2. Christy Breeze
3. Christmas
4. Christopher
5. Chris
6. christen
7. chords
8. schedule
9. anchor
10. chrome
11. stomach
12. ache
13. chorus

ss = sh

14. mission
15. admission
16. permission
17. discussion

"Hi, Mom! School's out! I'm home! Christmas vacation is here at last! Hooray!"

Christopher was going on vacation. No more school till after Christmas. He would have fun!

He would go on a ship with his folks. It was a big, new ship. Chris and Dad saw Mom christen it.

I christen you, The Christy Breeze!

THE CHRISTY BRE

Chris said,
 "Most ships have girls' names, but I like it anyway."

Then the band struck up the chords of The Star-Spangled Banner. Chris stood at attention and sang.

Then there was a big party. There were lots of Christmas cookies. Chris had a good time.

Start the engines!

Full Power!

We're set to sail!

Soon Captain Hank shouted, "Is everyone ready? We must leave on schedule. The tide is going out."

Rumble, rumble, went the big engines.

Up came
the big anchor.

Toot, toot! went the big whistle. Out into the harbor went The Christy Breeze out into the sea...right on schedule.

There were many things to do on the ship...even a movie theater, with no admission charge!

There were three dining rooms! Chris gave himself a mission...he would try every one!

First, Chris went to the Snack Bar. It was a fancy place with lots of chrome. Chris had a lemon soda.

Next, Chris played ping pong with his dad. That was fun, but it was a long session. It made Chris thirsty.

Chris had a root beer soda. Then he began to play shuffle board.

On and on sailed The Christy Breeze, over the big waves in the sea.

"I feel funny," said Chris.
"I feel fuzzy and green.
I have a stomach ache."

29

Mom put Chris to bed.
Dad got the ship's doctor.
They had a short discussion.

"No more sodas without permission. Take these pills. Soon you will feel fine again."

And soon Chris did feel fine.

He had a perfect Christmas. What a big Christmas tree was on The Christy Breeze!

The children made a chorus. They sang Christmas carols. The had a big Christmas wreath.

Captain Hank's present was the best. He let each child come up to the bridge of the ship.

CAPTAIN'S CABIN

Chris had permission to steer The Christy Breeze and wear the Captain's hat! What a Christmas it was!

The End

Raceway Step 35a

Rulebreakers and **Wacky Words**

Brave Heart, the Indian Guide

Vocabulary

1. heart
2. guide
3. ocean
4. shoes
5. any
6. very
7. many
8. sure
9. picture
10. friends
11. once
12. pneumonia
13. busy
14. come
15. sugar
16. Wednesday
17. lĭve
18. knows
19. early
20. two
21. why
22. from
23. again
24. answer
25. does

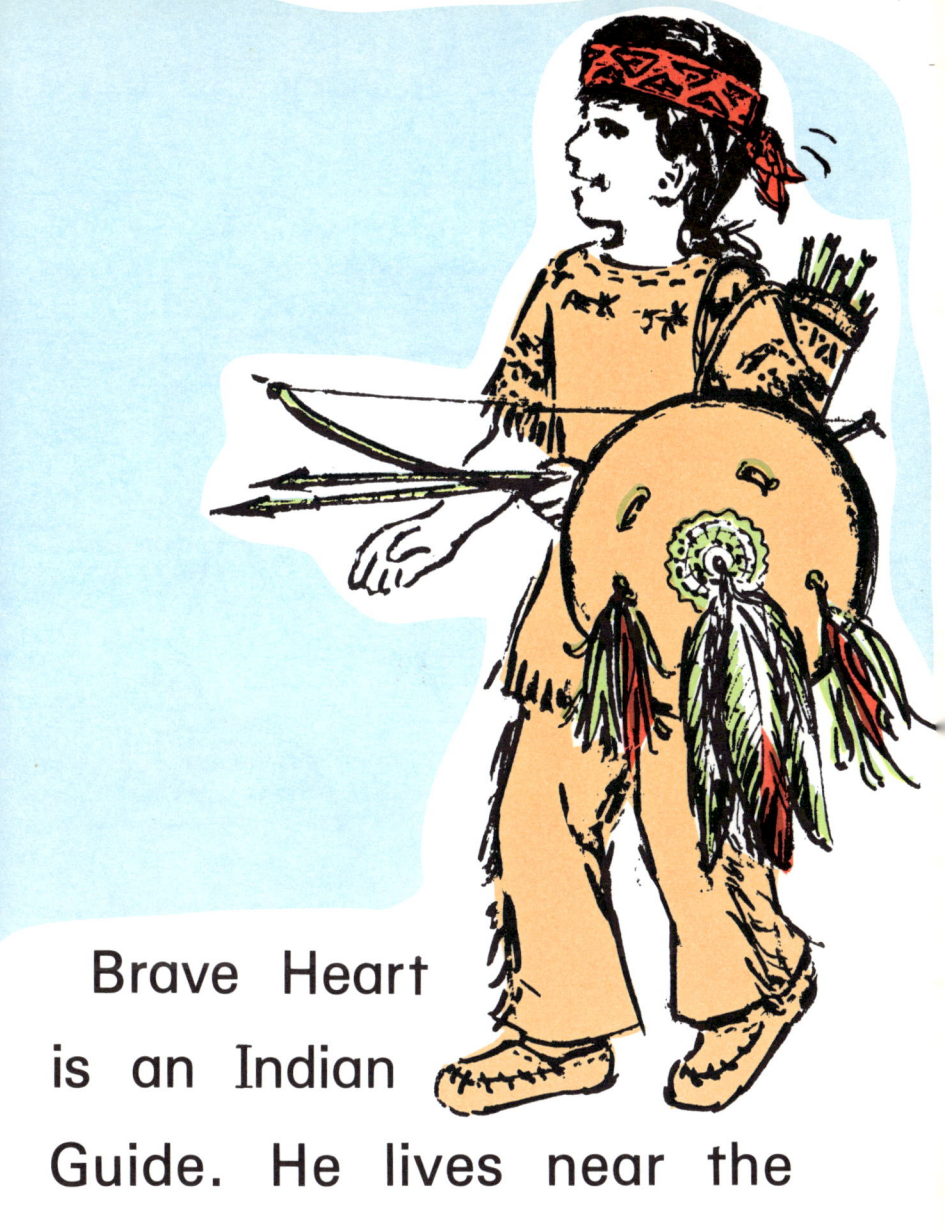

Brave Heart is an Indian Guide. He lives near the ocean. When he walks in the forest, his shoes don't make any noise.

Brave Heart is very clever.

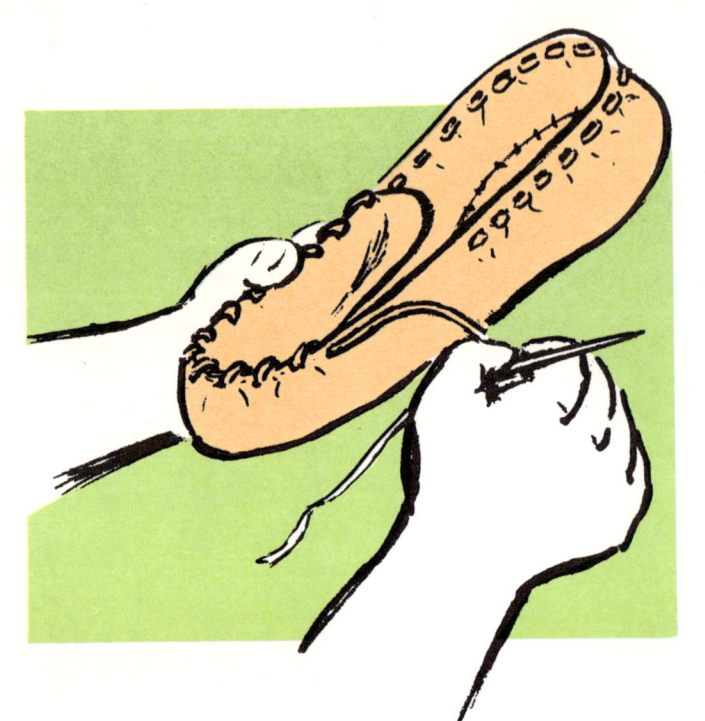

Brave Heart can make his own shoes. They are very soft shoes. They are made of leather.

Brave Heart knows many things.

He knows which berry is medicine, and which is poison. He knows which bird sings and which does not.

How many living things do you see in this picture?

Answer: There are ten besides Brave Heart.

He is sure of all
the paths
in the
woods.

He likes all the animals in the woods. They are his friends. There are eleven of them here. **Can you find them?**

Once on a Wednesday, in early Spring, two deer came to Brave Heart.

Do not be afraid.

Come, I will try to help.

One deer was sick. It had pneumonia.

"She has come to me for help," said Brave Heart to himself.

41

Brave Heart got busy. He made a strong medicine from berries and the roots of plants.

The next Wednesday, Brave Heart said, "Your mate is well again."

"Come, we will show you your reward," the deer seemed to answer. They led Brave Heart into the forest.

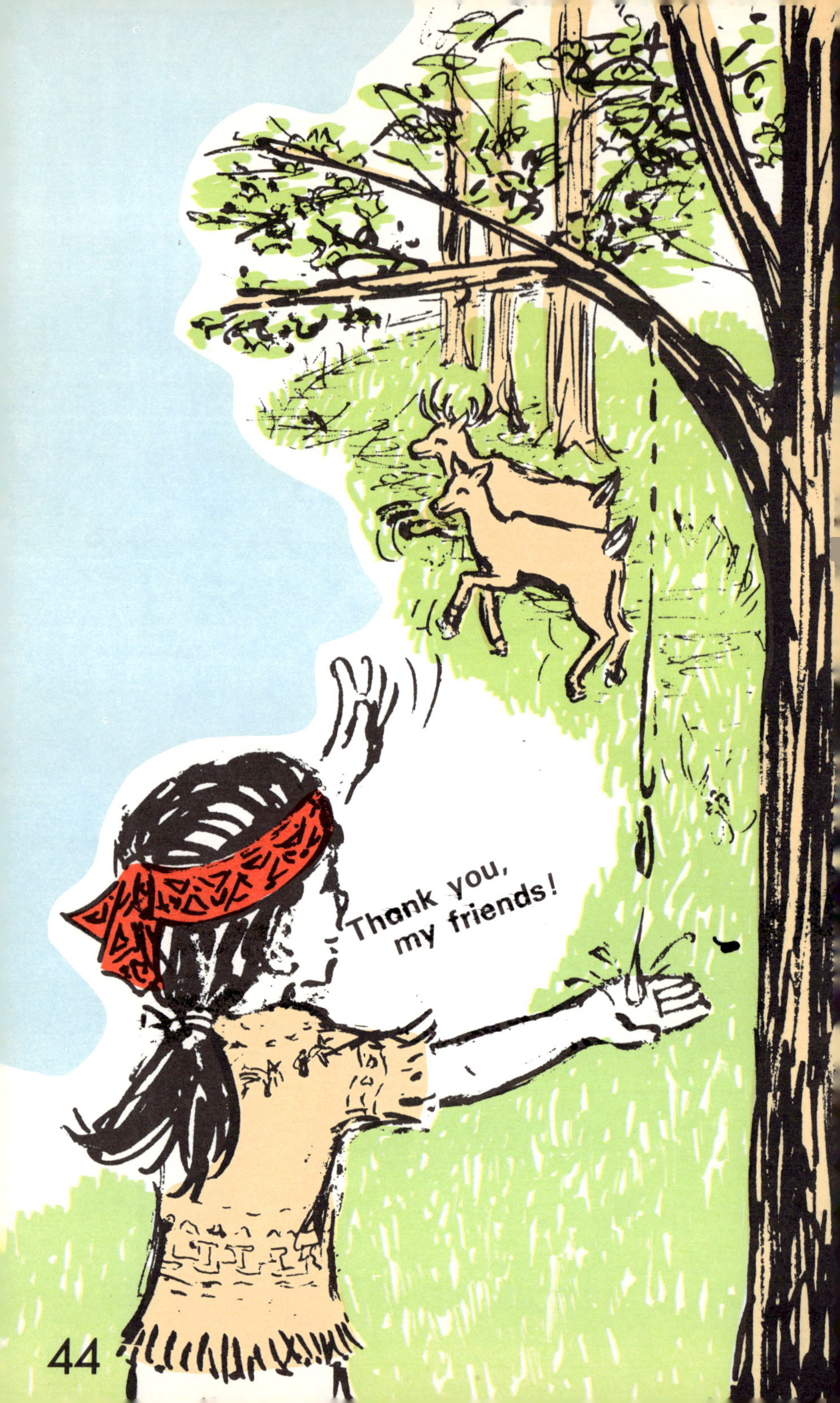
Thank you,
my friends!

The two deer showed Brave Heart a big tree. It was a maple tree. Sap was dripping from it.

"Mmm, it is sweet. I will cook it to make maple syrup. Mmmm! Maple sugar, too! Thank you, my friends!"

The End

Raceway 35b
Rulebreakers
and
Wacky Words

Friends

Vocabulary

1. many
2. hearts
3. eyes
4. pizza
5. some
6. soup
7. sure
8. four
9. friends
10. colonel
11. lieutenant
12. sergeants
13. built
14. easy
15. work

Four friends can have fun.
They can play together.

Tim, Ed, Sally, and Ann were friends. They liked to play Secret Spy.

Tim was the biggest. He was the colonel.

Ann was the lieutenant.

Ed and Sally were sergeants.

48

Ed and Ann built a fire. Tim and Sally cooked soup for lunch. It is easy if you all work together.

They went on a hike in the woods. They climbed on some rocks. Then they saw some tracks!

After that, they played Secret Spy.

Then they heard many noises! Their hearts began to go "Thump thump!"

51

"Oh, Nat! You sure did fool us! We are so glad it's you!"

Soon it was time to go home.

Tim's dad was at the door. "Where have you been?" he asked. "Mom has some pizza for your friends. Hot from the stove!"

"Yippee!"

The End

53

Raceway Step 36

ch = sh

The Move to Chicago

Vocabulary

1. Charlotte
2. Michelle
3. Cheryl
4. Chalfonte
5. Chicago
6. Chevrolet
7. Michigan
8. Chopin
11. chalet
12. chaise
13. chandelier
14. chef
15. parachute
16. crochet
17. chartreuse

Charlotte, Michelle, and Cheryl Chalfonte are so happy. They are moving to Chicago! Dad will drive the family there in their chartreuse Chevrolet. Their chalet home in Michigan had been sold.

The family watched as the movers loaded the van. In went the chaise lounge. In went the dining-room chandelier. In went Dad's chef hat!

In went Michelle's toy parachute!

"Dad will be our grand chauffeur," Mom teased, as they packed the car. "We will listen to his Chopin music tapes along the way, and I will crochet a new scarf. "That will be fun," said Dad. Everyone agreed.

Moving to Chicago from Michigan was a great event for the Chalfonte family.

The End

Have you ever moved? Why don't you write a story about it?

Raceway 36

ous
and
multi-syllable words

The Enormous Surprise

Vocabulary

1. curious
2. enormous
3. cafeteria
4. yesterday
5. tomorrow
6. fabulous
7. serious
8. explanation
9. detective
10. apartment
11. elevator
12. subtraction
13. together
14. investigation
15. dangerous
16. location
17. generous
18. gorgeous
19. celebrate
20. minute (minit)

Bob was curious. **What** was going on in the cafeteria? Yesterday they had locked the door. No one could come in. Not until tomorrow! What **was** that fabulous smell? It made Bob hungry.

57

"I'll get the famous Detective Dick. He is sure to find an explanation."

Bob took the elevator to the apartment where Dick lives with his mom and dad.

Dick was doing subtraction.

"Let's go together," said Bob. "This smell needs investigation."

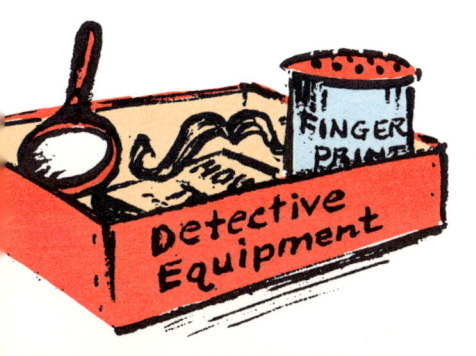

"Let me see what I'll need," said Dick.

59

"It might be dangerous! Be careful!" called Bob.

"I'll call the fire department, and give our location!"

"What's all the commotion? Call off the fire engines. You boys are too curious! But I will be generous... come on inside," said the cook.

"What an enormous cake! It's gorgeous!" cried Bob and Dick. "We can't believe our eyes!"

"It is for Mrs. Dickson's class," said the cook. "You will know why tomorrow."

"Yippee! That's our class!" yelled Bob and Dick together.

Now boys and girls, **you** have a celebration too! You can read **anything** now! Isn't that fabulous?

Congratulations !!!

The End